blue zoo guides

mammals

by Dee Phillips

TWO CAN™

Published in North America in 2006 by Two-Can Publishing
11571 K-Tel Drive, Minnetonka, MN 55343
www.two-canpublishing.com

Copyright © ticktock Entertainment Ltd 2006
First published in Great Britain in 2005 by ticktock Media Ltd.,
Unit 2, Orchard Business Centre, North Farm Road, Tunbridge Wells, Kent, TN2 3XF

Library of Congress Cataloging-in Publication Data

Phillips, Dee, 1967-
Mammals / by Dee Phillips.
p. cm. -- (Blue zoo guides)
Summary: "Introduces mammals from around the world, including information about
where they live, what they eat, and how they grow and survive"--Provided by publisher.
Includes index.
ISBN 1-58728-519-3 (reinforced hc)
1. Mammals—Juvenile literature. I. Title. II. Series.
QL706.2.P55 2006
599—dc22   2005017711

1 2 3 4 5 10 09 08 07 06

Printed in China

Contents

Meet the Mammals	4
The Wide World of Animals	6
Anteater	8
Antelope	10
Arctic Hare	12
Baboon	14
Beaver	16
Blue Whale	18
Buffalo	20
Camel	22
Cheetah	24
Chimpanzee	26
Dolphin	28
Duck-Billed Platypus	30
Elephant	32
Fruit Bat	34
Giant Panda	36
Giraffe	38
Gorilla	40
Grizzly Bear	42
Hippopotamus	44
Kangaroo	46
Koala	48
Lemur	50
Leopard	52
Lion	54
Mandrill	56
Meerkat	58
Moose	60
Orangutan	62
Orca	64
Otter	66
Polar Bear	68
Porcupine	70
Raccoon	72
Reindeer	74
Rhinoceros	76
Seal	78
Snow Monkey	80
Tamarin	82
Tiger	84
Walrus	86
Warthog	88
Wolf	90
Zebra	92
Glossary	94
Index	96

Words that appear in **bold** are explained in the glossary.

Meet the Mammals

The word **mammal** describes many of the animals that you know.

The fierce lion, the huge elephant, and the tall giraffe are all mammals. So how do you tell if an animal is a mammal?

• Mammals give birth to live babies.

• Mammal babies drink milk from their mothers' bodies.

• Most mammals have a hairy or furry body.

Mammal Menus

Some mammals, such as tigers and seals, eat only meat or fish. Other mammals, like giraffes and camels, eat only plants. But many mammals, such as grizzly bears and baboons, like to eat meat AND plants!

Look for these pictures, and they will tell you what kind of food each animal eats.

Plants

**Meat
(including insects
and worms)**

**Fish and
Shellfish**

The Wide World of Animals

The map on this page shows our world.

The blue areas on the map are oceans. The other colors show large areas of land called continents. North America and Africa are continents. Some of the animals you'll meet in this book live in more than one continent. Other animals in this book live in just one continent, or just one part of a continent.

When you read about an animal in this book, see if you can find the place where they live on the map. Can you find where YOU live?

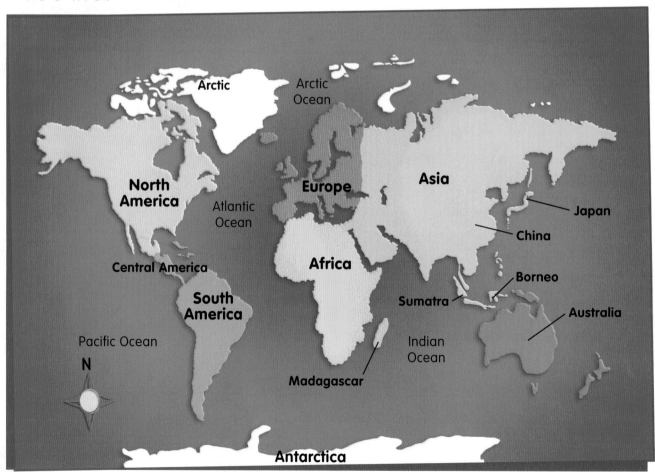

Mammal Habitats

Some animals live in hot, wet forests. Others live in cold, salty oceans. The different kinds of places where animals live are called **habitats.**

Look for these pictures in your book, and they will tell you what kind of habitat each animal needs to survive.

Deserts – hot, dry, sandy places where it hardly ever rains

Hardwood forests – forests with trees that lose their leaves in winter

Polar lands – cold, frozen places at the very top and bottom of the earth

Mountains – high, rocky places

Evergreen forests – cool forests with trees that stay green all year

Grasslands – dry places covered with grass

Fresh water – lakes, ponds, **wetlands,** rivers, or streams

Rain forests – hot, wet forests with very tall trees

Oceans – huge areas of deep, salty water

Anteater

Anteaters live in South America and Central America. Some anteaters live in forests. This giant anteater lives on grasslands.

Giant anteaters have long snouts for sniffing out ant nests.

A mother anteater carries her baby on her back. Sometimes she wraps her furry tail around it to keep it warm.

3 ft	6 ft	9 ft	12 ft
0.9 m	1.8 m	2.7 m	3.7 m

Anteaters eat ants and **termites**.
They tear open the insects'
nests with long, sharp claws.

A giant anteater's tongue can be up to
24 inches (60 cm) long! It uses
this handy tool to lap
up thousands of
tiny insects
every day.

Antelope

Antelope live on the grasslands of Africa and Asia. They can run fast and jump high. Some can even swim!

There are many different kinds of antelope. Some are big and some are small.

An antelope's horns can be long or short, twisted or straight.

This is a kob antelope.

15 ft
4.6 m

12 ft
3.7 m

9 ft
2.7 m

6 ft
1.8 m

3 ft
0.9 m

These antelope are springboks. The baby is called a calf. It drinks milk. When it grows up, it will eat grass and leaves like its mother does.

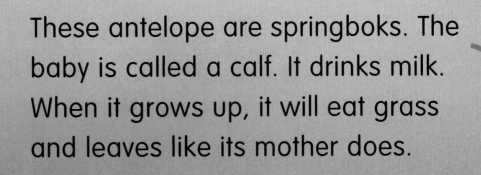

Antelope have hard, tough feet called hooves for running fast.

Arctic Hare

Arctic hares live in the cold and snow of the Arctic and in the top part of North America. They eat grass, **moss,** and other plants.

black ear tips

a thick, warm coat

In summer, the arctic hare has brown fur. When winter comes, its coat turns white. This helps the hare to blend in with the snow and hide from **predators.**

3 ft
0.9 m

6 ft
1.8 m

Baby hares are called leverets.

Arctic hares can run very fast to escape from a predator.

Baboon

15 ft
4.6 m

12 ft
3.7 m

Baboons are large monkeys. There are five kinds of baboons. They live in Africa and west Asia, in many different habitats.

9 ft
2.7 m

Baboons live on the ground in large groups called troops.

6 ft
1.8 m

Baboon babies ride on their mothers' backs.

3 ft
0.9 m

Baboons eat leaves, roots, seeds, fruit, birds' eggs, bugs, and even lizards!

14

Male baboons bark to warn the troop if there is danger.

These big cheeks are handy for carrying food.

Beaver

Beavers are large **rodents.** They live near rivers, streams, lakes, ponds, and wetlands in North America, Europe, and Asia.

Baby beavers are called kits or pups.

Beavers eat branches, leaves, and tree **bark.**

3 ft
0.9 m

6 ft
1.8 m

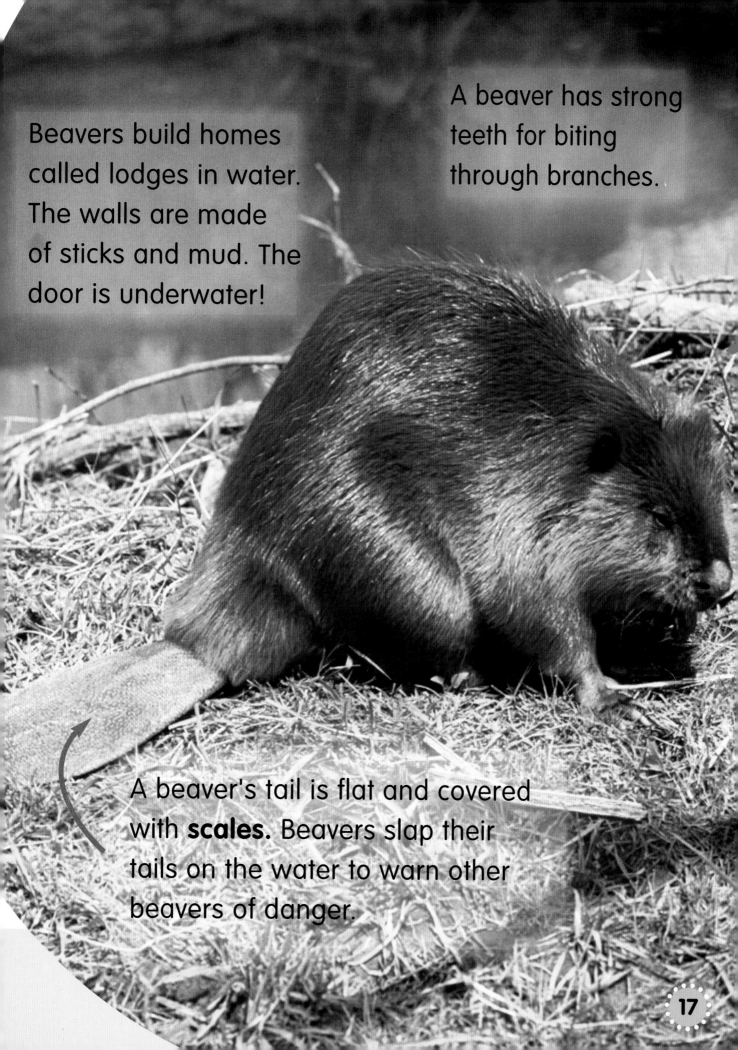

Beavers build homes called lodges in water. The walls are made of sticks and mud. The door is underwater!

A beaver has strong teeth for biting through branches.

A beaver's tail is flat and covered with **scales.** Beavers slap their tails on the water to warn other beavers of danger.

Blue Whale

Blue whales are the **largest** animals that have ever lived. They are found in all the oceans of the world.

Blue whales make a whistling noise that is louder than a jet plane!

A blue whale's heart is the same size as a small car!

30 ft
9 m

60 ft
18 m

90 ft
27 m

120 ft
36 m

Every day, blue whales eat millions of tiny shrimp called krill.

Flippers help push a whale to the surface.

The strong tail is made up of two flukes.

A baby blue whale is called a calf.

Buffalo

Buffalo are **big**, heavy animals with hard feet called hooves. They live in hot places in Africa and Asia.

Sharp horns protect a buffalo from predators.

15 ft
4.6 m

12 ft
3.7 m

9 ft
2.7 m

6 ft
1.8 m

3 ft
0.9 m

They live in huge **herds** on grasslands. Asian buffalo also live on wetlands. They cool down in the water when it gets too hot.

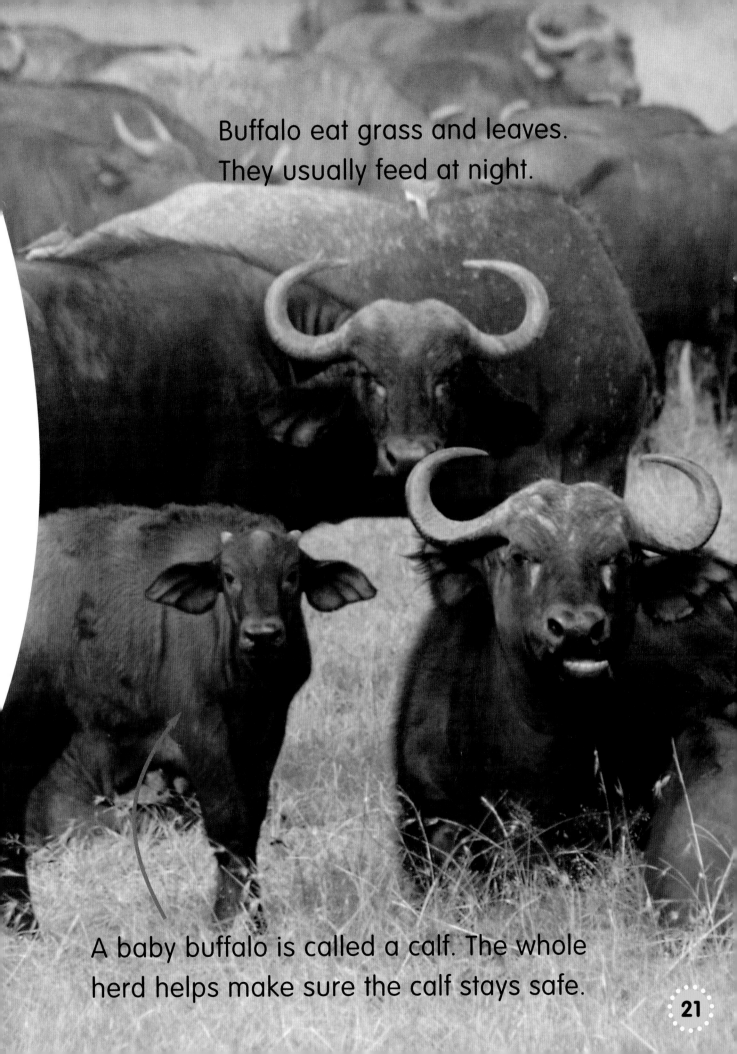

Buffalo eat grass and leaves.
They usually feed at night.

A baby buffalo is called a calf. The whole
herd helps make sure the calf stays safe.

15 ft
4.6 m

12 ft
3.7 m

9 ft
2.7 m

Camel

Camels live in the sandy deserts of Africa and Asia. They have special noses and eyelashes that keep out blowing sand.

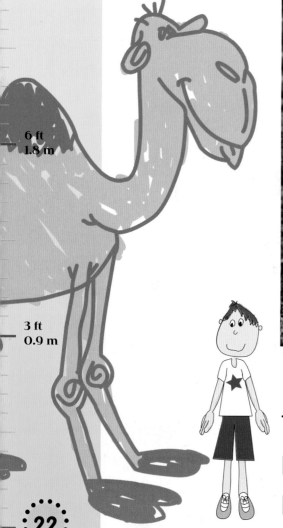

A baby camel is called a calf.

Camels eat grass and plants.

6 ft
1.8 m

3 ft
0.9 m

There are two types of camels. Bactrian camels have two humps. Dromedaries have one hump.

A camel can go without water for almost two weeks!

Camels store fat in their humps. They use the fat for energy when there is no food.

23

Cheetah

Cheetahs live on grasslands in Africa and west Asia. They are the fastest of all the land animals!

These long legs are made for running.

Cheetahs hunt and eat antelope and small, quick animals such as rabbits.

When cheetahs chase their **prey,** they can run as fast as a car on a highway!

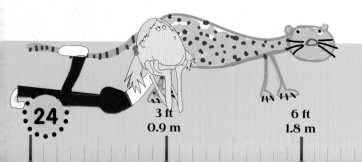

| 3 ft | 6 ft | 9 ft | 12 ft |
| 0.9 m | 1.8 m | 2.7 m | 3.7 m |

This spotted fur
helps the cheetah
to hide in long
grass and bushes.

Baby cheetahs
are called cubs.

Chimpanzee

Chimpanzees are **apes.** They live in forests in Africa. Chimps eat fruit, leaves, and bugs, such as ants and termites.

Chimpanzees walk on all fours. Their arms are longer than their legs.

Chimps make faces to show other chimps that they are happy, scared, or angry!

15 ft
4.6 m

12 ft
3.7 m

9 ft
2.7 m

6 ft
1.8 m

3 ft
0.9 m

Chimps live in family groups of six to ten animals.

A mother chimp feeds, **grooms,** and carries her baby until it is three or four years old.

Dolphin

Dolphins are mammals that live in all the world's oceans, and in some rivers. There are 36 different kinds of dolphins. The biggest of these is the orca.

Dolphins eat fish and **shellfish**.

dorsal fin

smooth, rubbery skin

flipper

beak with lots of sharp teeth

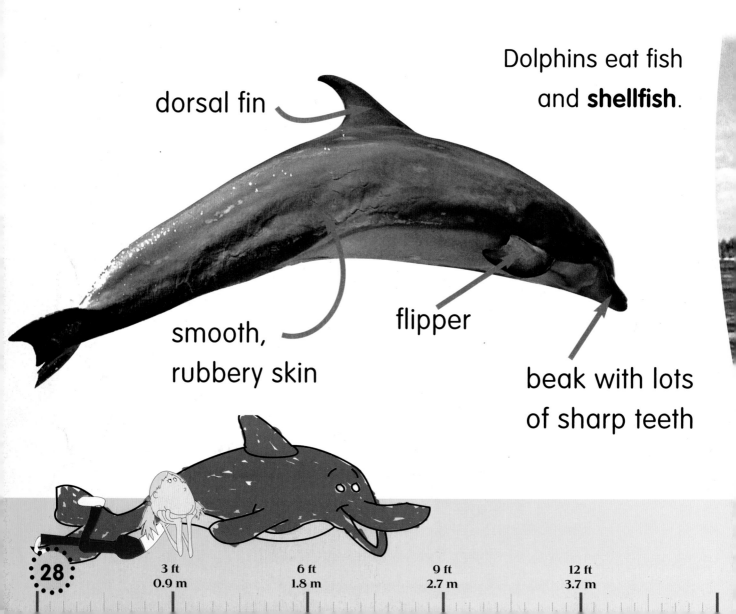

| 3 ft 0.9 m | 6 ft 1.8 m | 9 ft 2.7 m | 12 ft 3.7 m |

A baby dolphin is called a calf. It takes quick drinks of milk from its mother as it swims.

These playful bottlenose dolphins can leap high into the air!

Dolphins live in groups called pods. They talk to each other using squeaks and clicks.

Duck-Billed Platypus

Duck-billed platypuses live in ponds and small rivers in Australia. They eat shellfish, worms, insects, and snails.

Duck-billed platypuses are very unusual mammals because they lay eggs!

When the eggs **hatch**, the mother platypus feeds the babies milk. Baby platypuses are called puggles.

3 ft
0.9 m

6 ft
1.8 m

Duck-billed platypuses live in **burrows** dug into riverbanks.

They have a flat mouth, shaped like a duck's beak.

They have **waterproof** fur and **webbed** feet for swimming.

Elephant

The elephant is the **biggest** land animal on earth. African elephants live on grasslands. Asian elephants live in forests.

Elephant mothers and babies live in groups called herds.

A baby elephant is called a calf.

3 ft	6 ft	9 ft	12 ft
0.9 m	1.8 m	2.7 m	3.7 m

Elephants eat grass, leaves, roots, branches, bark, and fruit.

Every day, they drink enough water to fill a bathtub!

Elephants use their trunks for smelling, picking up food, and sucking up water.

These HUGE teeth are called tusks.

Fruit Bat

Bats are mammals that fly! There are hundreds of different kinds. Fruit bats are larger than other bats and have big eyes.

Fruit bats live in the rain forests of Africa, Europe, Asia, and Australia.

A baby fruit bat is called a pup.

Fruit bats come in many sizes.

3 ft	6 ft	9 ft	12 ft
0.9 m	1.8 m	2.7 m	3.7 m

Fruit bats eat the soft parts of a fruit and drink the juice.

A bat can fold up its wings.

This fruit bat is called a flying fox.

Fruit bats use their sharp eyesight to search for food at night. During the day, they sleep upside down!

Giant Panda

Giant pandas live in just one small part of China, a country in Asia. They live high in the mountains in cold, wet forests.

Pandas eat a tough plant called bamboo. They hold the stems in their front paws.

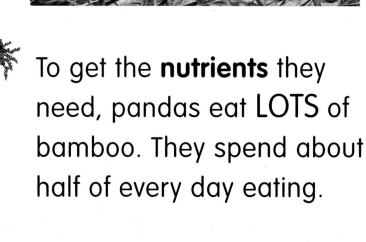

To get the **nutrients** they need, pandas eat LOTS of bamboo. They spend about half of every day eating.

15 ft
4.6 m

12 ft
3.7 m

9 ft
2.7 m

6 ft
1.8 m

3 ft
0.9 m

A young panda is called a cub.

A newborn cub is blind and hairless. It is not much bigger than a candy bar!

Giraffe

Giraffes are the **tallest** animals in the world. They live on grasslands in Africa.

Giraffes eat leaves and twigs.

A giraffe's long neck helps it to reach the tops of trees. It grabs the leaves with its long, black tongue.

15 ft
4.6 m

12 ft
3.7 m

9 ft
2.7 m

6 ft
1.8 m

3 ft
0.9 m

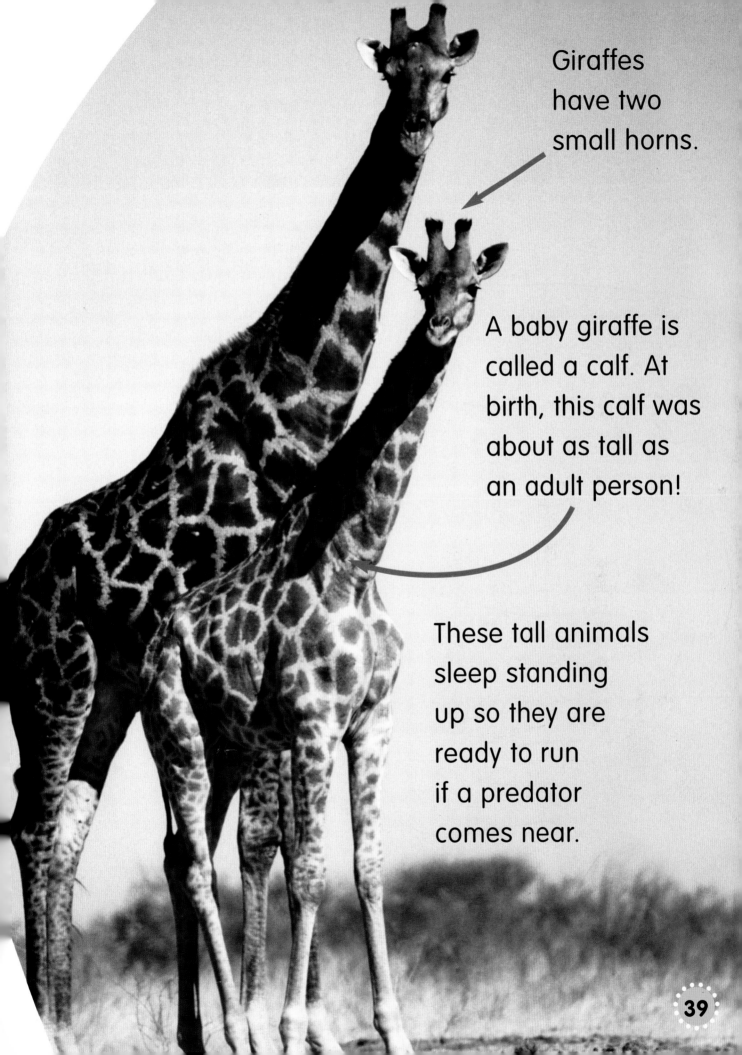

Giraffes have two small horns.

A baby giraffe is called a calf. At birth, this calf was about as tall as an adult person!

These tall animals sleep standing up so they are ready to run if a predator comes near.

Gorilla

Gorillas are the **biggest** of all the **apes.** They live in the rain forests of Africa. Gorillas eat plants and fruit.

Adult male gorillas have a patch of light-colored fur on their backs. They are called silverbacks.

Gorillas live in family groups called troops. The silverback is the leader.

15 ft
4.6 m

12 ft
3.7 m

9 ft
2.7 m

6 ft
1.8 m

3 ft
0.9 m

40

Adult gorillas teach the babies how to find food.

At night, gorillas build nests of branches and leaves to sleep in.

Gorillas are gentle and very smart. Baby gorillas like to play!

Grizzly Bear

Bears are big, heavy mammals with thick, hairy coats. Grizzly bears live in mountains and forests in some parts of North America.

Baby grizzlies are called cubs. They live with their mothers until they are three or four years old.

Grizzly bears eat plants, meat, and sometimes fish.

| 3 ft 0.9 m | 6 ft 1.8 m | 9 ft 2.7 m | 12 ft 3.7 m |

Bears have large, long snouts that help them sniff out food!

Grizzly bears spend the cold winter months sleeping in cozy **dens,** caves, or hollow logs.

43

Hippopotamus

Hippopotamuses live in lakes, rivers, and wetlands in Africa. They have **huge** mouths and teeth, and they can be very fierce.

Baby hippos are born underwater. They can weigh up to 110 pounds (50 kg).

A baby hippo is called a calf.

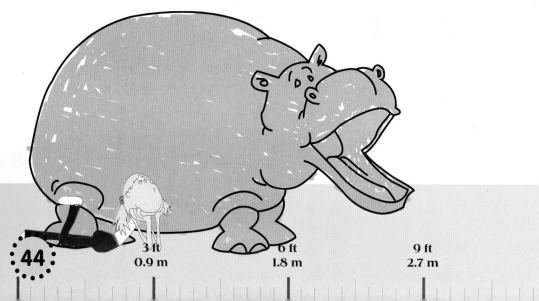

3 ft	6 ft	9 ft	12 ft
0.9 m	1.8 m	2.7 m	3.7 m

A hippo can close its nostrils to keep water out of its nose!

Hippos live in large herds.

Hippos spend most of the day in the water. At night, they come on shore to find grass to eat.

15 ft
4.6 m

12 ft
3.7 m

9 ft
2.7 m

6 ft
1.8 m

3 ft
0.9 m

Kangaroo

Kangaroos live on grasslands and in forests in Australia.

Kangaroos hop very fast using their big, strong back legs.

Their tails help them to balance as they hop.

A baby kangaroo lives and grows in a special **pouch** on the front of its mother's body. Animals that raise babies this way are called **marsupials.**

Kangaroos eat
grass and plants.

A baby kangaroo is
called a joey. It gets
a bouncy ride in its
mother's pouch.

Koala

Koalas live in Australia. They live in eucalyptus trees and eat the tree's leaves. Like kangaroos, koalas are marsupials.

Baby koalas are called joeys.

A newborn koala is very tiny. It lives in its mother's pouch for six months. Then it rides on her back until it can climb on its own.

Koalas sleep for up to 20 hours each day!

This thick, woolly coat protects the koala from rain and cold.

Koalas have claws and rough pads on their feet for gripping branches.

Lemur

Lemurs are related to monkeys and apes.
They live on the island of Madagascar.

Some kinds of lemurs are as small as mice. This ring-tailed lemur is about the size of a cat.

striped tail

A baby lemur holds on tight to its mother's back as she leaps through the trees.

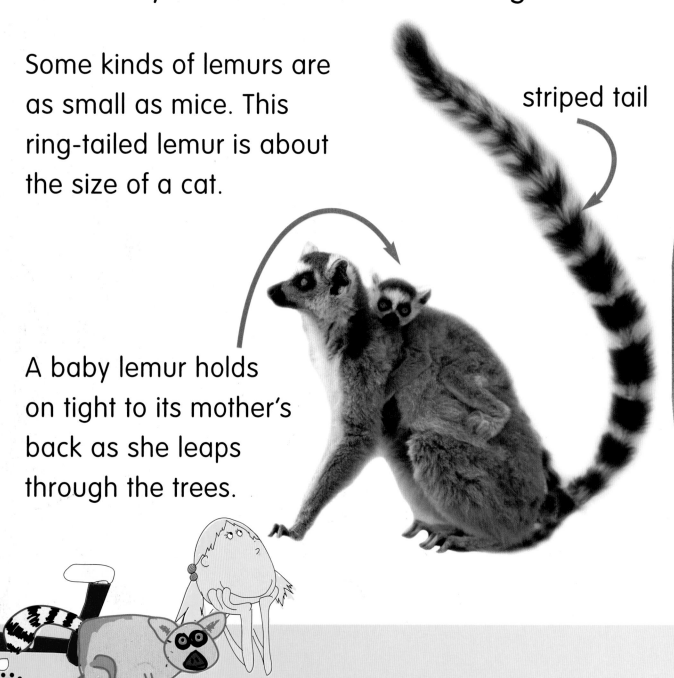

3 ft
0.9 m

6 ft
1.8 m

Lemurs eat mostly fruit and plants. Some lemurs also eat birds' eggs, insects, and other small animals.

Ring-tailed lemurs live on the ground and in trees.

Leopard

Leopards are big cats. They live on grasslands and in deserts and forests in Africa and Asia.

Baby leopards are called cubs. They live with their mothers until they are about two years old.

Adult leopards live alone. They often sleep and eat in trees.

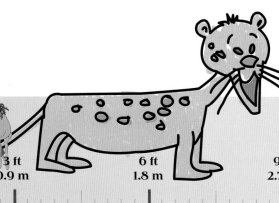

3 ft
0.9 m

6 ft
1.8 m

9 ft
2.7 m

12 ft
3.7 m

Leopards hunt many different animals, from birds and baboons to big antelope. They do most of their hunting at night.

Lion

Lions are big, strong cats. They live in family groups called prides. Lions are found on grasslands in Africa.

The male lion has a thick, furry mane.

Females are called lionesses.

A male lion's **ROAR** can be heard 5 miles (8 km) away.

| 3 ft | 6 ft | 9 ft | 12 ft |
| 0.9 m | 1.8 m | 2.7 m | 3.7 m |

Lion families work together
to hunt zebras, antelope,
and buffalo.

This is a lion **cub.**
The lionesses in a
pride help
each other
take care
of their
cubs.

Mandrill

Mandrills are the **biggest** members of the monkey family. They live in the rain forests of Africa.

A baby mandrill holds on tight to its mother as they explore the forest.

Mandrills eat mostly seeds and fruit. They also eat eggs, insects, and small animals. They carry any extra food in their cheeks!

15 ft
4.6 m

12 ft
3.7 m

9 ft
2.7 m

6 ft
1.8 m

3 ft
0.9 m

Mandrill families spend all day searching for food on the ground. At night, they sleep in trees.

Male mandrills have red and blue faces.

Meerkat

Meerkats live on grasslands in Africa. Large groups of meerkats live together in underground burrows.

Baby meerkats are called pups.

One adult meerkat babysits all the pups while the rest of the group goes out to look for food.

Meerkats take turns standing guard outside the burrow. They call out a warning if they see a predator.

15 ft
4.6 m

12 ft
3.7 m

9 ft
2.7 m

6 ft
1.8 m

3 ft
0.9 m

Meerkats eat mostly insects. They also eat small animals such as lizards and mice.

These long claws are made to dig burrows and to scratch in the dirt for bugs.

Moose

15 ft
4.6 m

12 ft
3.7 m

9 ft
2.7 m

6 ft
1.8 m

3 ft
0.9 m

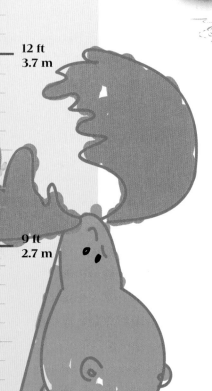

Moose live in forests in North America, Europe, and Asia. They are the **biggest** members of the deer family.

A baby moose is called a calf.

Moose eat twigs and tree bark in the winter. In the summer, they wade in lakes to find water plants and keep cool.

Moose are fast runners and very good swimmers.

A male moose has huge **antlers.** They fall off in the winter and grow back in the spring.

Orangutan

Orangutans live in rain forests on the islands of Borneo and Sumatra, in Asia. They are found high in the treetops.

Baby orangutans ride along with their mothers until they are about three years old.

Long arms help them swing through the trees.

Orangutans eat fruit. Mothers chew up their babies' food to make it easier to eat.

15 ft
4.6 m

12 ft
3.7 m

9 ft
2.7 m

6 ft
1.8 m

3 ft
0.9 m

Male orangutans have large, soft cheek pads that feel like leather.

Orangutans are very clever. They use leaves as umbrellas when it rains!

Orca

Orcas are a kind of dolphin. They live in all the world's oceans. These huge mammals can swim very fast to catch their prey.

Orcas live in big family groups called pods. Calves stay with their mother their whole life.

A baby orca is called a calf.

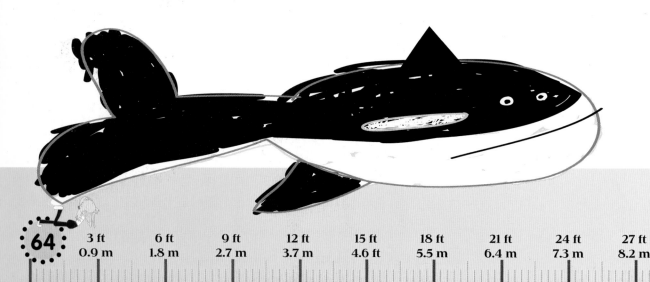

3 ft	6 ft	9 ft	12 ft	15 ft	18 ft	21 ft	24 ft	27 ft
0.9 m	1.8 m	2.7 m	3.7 m	4.6 ft	5.5 m	6.4 m	7.3 m	8.2 m

An orca's dorsal fin may be 6 feet (1.8 m) tall.

Thick **blubber** keeps the animal warm in icy water.

Orcas eat fish, birds, seals, and even sharks!

Otter

Most kinds of otters live in rivers and lakes around the world. They are called river otters. Sea otters live in the Pacific Ocean.

Sea otters eat fish and shellfish. They open clam shells by cracking them on a rock!

Baby otters are called cubs or pups. Otter families love to chase and play together.

3 ft
0.9 m

6 ft
1.8 m

Otters are very good swimmers. They have waterproof fur and webbed feet.

Sea otters have thicker fur than any other animal. They groom themselves for several hours every day!

Polar Bear

Polar bears live in the Arctic on icy, cold land and on huge patches of frozen ocean. They have thick fur and blubber to keep warm.

A baby polar bear is called a cub. Mother polar bears dig dens in the snow where they give birth to their cubs.

A polar bear's main food is seals.

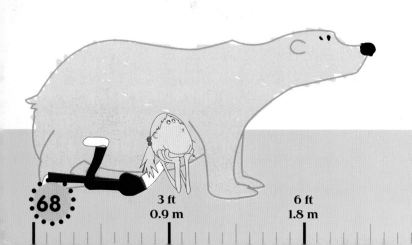

| 3 ft | 6 ft | 9 ft | 12 ft |
| 0.9 m | 1.8 m | 2.7 m | 3.7 m |

Polar bears can
smell food that is
many miles away!

These paws are
as big as
dinner plates!

Porcupine

Porcupines are rodents that live in North America, South America, and Africa. They are covered in sharp spikes called quills.

These quills protect the porcupine from predators.

African porcupines make their homes among rocks or in small caves.

3 ft	6 ft	9 ft	12 ft
0.9 m	1.8 m	2.7 m	3.7 m

Porcupines' teeth never stop growing! Chewing on tough materials such as bark wears them down.

Porcupines eat mostly plants, roots, berries, and nuts.

North American porcupines may climb trees to find food.

Raccoon

Raccoons live in many different habitats in North America. They are sometimes called northern raccoons.

A baby raccoon is called a kit.

Raccoons eat lots of foods, including insects, nuts, berries, and frogs. They will even steal leftovers from trash cans!

| 3 ft | 6 ft | 9 ft | 12 ft |
| 0.9 m | 1.8 m | 2.7 m | 3.7 m |

Its striped tail helps the raccoon blend into the forest.

Raccoons can use their little hands to open doors, turn on faucets, and even open soda cans!

Reindeer

Reindeer are a type of deer. They live in forests and in snowy, icy places at the very top of North America, Europe, and Asia. They are also known as caribou.

Reindeer live in big herds. Their babies are called calves.

In winter, reindeer dig in the snow with their hooves to find moss to eat.

3 ft	6 ft	9 ft	12 ft
0.9 m	1.8 m	2.7 m	3.7 m

In summer, reindeer eat grass and other plants.

Both males and females have antlers.

Thick brown fur keeps them warm in the winter.

Rhinoceros

Rhinos are HUGE mammals. They live in forests and on grasslands in Africa and Asia. Rhinos eat grasses and plants.

The two most common kinds are black rhinos and white rhinos. In spite of their names, all rhinos have gray skin.

A baby rhino is called a calf.

| 3 ft | 6 ft | 9 ft | 12 ft |
| 0.9 m | 1.8 m | 2.7 m | 3.7 m |

thick, tough skin

Rhinos cannot see
very well, but they
can smell and
hear well.

Some kinds of rhinos
have one horn.
Others have two.

Seal

There are many different kinds of seals. They live in oceans all over the world. Their main foods are fish, squid, and shellfish.

A baby seal is called a pup. Mother seals give birth to their pups on land or on huge chunks of floating ice.

This harp seal pup has white fur so predators cannot see him on the ice.

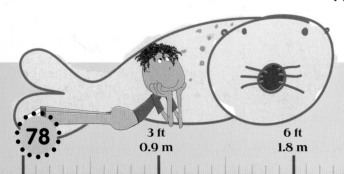

3 ft
0.9 m

6 ft
1.8 m

9 ft
2.7 m

12 ft
3.7 m

Seals are clumsy on land, but they are excellent swimmers and divers.

This is a gray seal.

Snow Monkey

Furry snow monkeys are found in the mountain forests of Japan, in Asia. They live in groups called troops.

These snow monkeys have found a great way to warm up. The pool they are soaking in is heated by water from deep in the earth.

Snow monkeys eat lots of fruit, as well as leaves, flowers, bark, and insects.

15 ft
4.6 m

12 ft
3.7 m

9 ft
2.7 m

6 ft
1.8 m

3 ft
0.9 m

Snow monkeys
have red faces
and thick, warm
coats.

Tamarin

Tamarins are small monkeys with long, soft fur. They live in the forests of South America.

Tamarins live in small family groups high in the treetops.

The parents and the older brothers and sisters all take turns carrying the babies.

3 ft
0.9 m

6 ft
1.8 m

9 ft
2.7 m

12 ft
3.7 m

This is a golden lion tamarin. Its silky mane makes it look like a little lion!

Tamarins eat insects, as well as fruit, seeds, and small animals.

Most monkeys have flat toenails, but tamarins have thin, sharp claws.

Tiger

Tigers are members of the cat family. They live in forests in Asia. Adult tigers normally live alone.

Tigers are most active at night. They hunt big animals such as deer and antelope.

Baby tigers are called cubs.

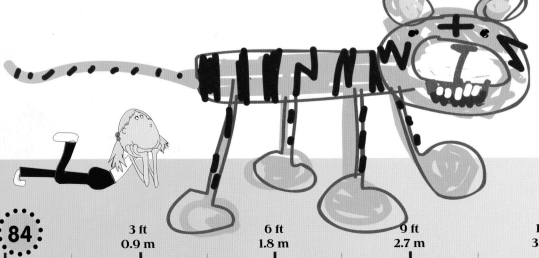

| 3 ft | 6 ft | 9 ft | 12 ft |
| 0.9 m | 1.8 m | 2.7 m | 3.7 m |

Some tigers live in hot places. Other tigers live in cold, snowy places.

Every tiger's stripes are different!

Walrus

Walruses are huge, heavy mammals.
They live in the Arctic, on land and in the water.

Walruses can stay underwater for 25 minutes, searching for shellfish, snails, and other small ocean animals.

A baby walrus is called a calf. Even at birth, it is one big baby!

| 3 ft | 6 ft | 9 ft | 12 ft |
| 0.9 m | 1.8 m | 2.7 m | 3.7 m |

Male walruses are much bigger than females in every way. That includes the tusks!

thick, wrinkly skin

Hundreds of walruses gather in a group called a rookery. They lie close together on a rocky beach or a large chunk of floating ice.

Warthog

Warthogs are a kind of wild pig. They live on grasslands in Africa. They have hard feet called hooves that help them to run fast.

Baby warthogs are called piglets. Mothers give birth to three or four piglets at one time.

Warthogs take mud baths to cool off when it is hot.

| 3 ft | 6 ft | 9 ft | 12 ft |
| 0.9 m | 1.8 m | 2.7 m | 3.7 m |

Warthogs eat grass, fruit, roots, bark, and dead animals.

They dig for roots using their strong snouts.

These tusks are used for fighting.

89

Wolf

Wolves live in forests in North America, Europe, and Asia. They live in small family groups called packs.

A baby wolf is called a pup or a cub. Mothers give birth to four to seven pups in a cozy den.

Wolves howl to tell others where they are. Howling also tells other wolf packs to stay away!

3 ft	6 ft	9 ft	12 ft
0.9 m	1.8 m	2.7 m	3.7 m

Wolf packs hunt big animals such as reindeer.

thick, warm fur

long, sharp teeth

Zebra

Zebras are wild relatives of horses. They live in herds on grasslands in Africa. Their main food is grass.

A baby zebra is called a foal. It can stand up just a few minutes after it is born!

15 ft
4.6 m

12 ft
3.7 m

9 ft
2.7 m

6 ft
1.8 m

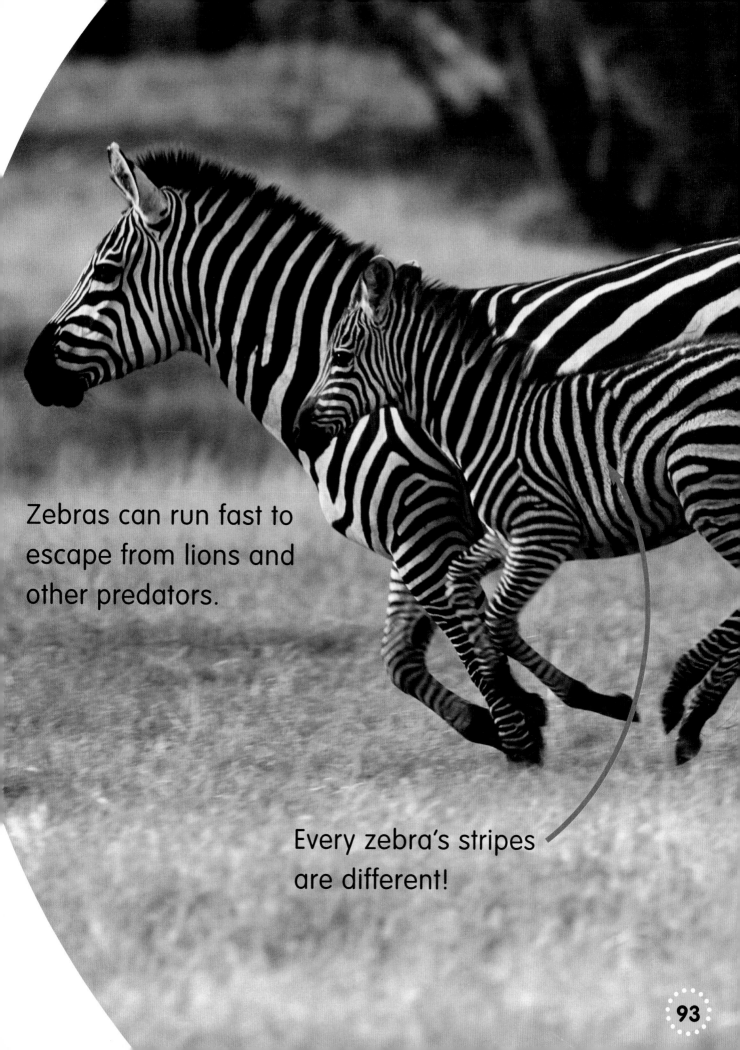

Zebras can run fast to escape from lions and other predators.

Every zebra's stripes are different!

Glossary

antlers: horn-like growths on the heads of some deer. These animals shed their antlers in the winter and grow new ones in the spring.

apes: a group of animals from the primate family. (Monkeys, humans, and lemurs are primates, too.) The biggest difference between apes and monkeys is their tails. Apes have short tails, or none at all.

bark: the tough, outer covering of a tree trunk or branch

blubber: a thick layer of fat under the skin

burrow: a hole or tunnel that an animal digs for shelter

den: a shelter for an animal, hidden in a log, a cave, or other hard-to-find spot

desert: a hot, dry place where it hardly ever rains. Only certain plants and animals can live there.

evergreen forest: a cool forest of trees with needle-like leaves that do not fall off in the autumn. It is also called a coniferous forest.

grasslands: dry places covered with grasses and dotted with a few bushes or trees

groom: to clean and take care of someone's appearance, especially their fur or hair

habitat: the place where an animal or plant makes its home, such as a desert or a pond

hardwood forest: a forest of trees whose leaves change color and fall off in the autumn. This kind of forest is also called a deciduous forest.

hatch: to be born by breaking out of an egg

herd: one name for a large group of animals

marsupials: mammals that carry their babies in a pouch until the babies are big enough to take care of themselves

monkeys: a group of animals from the primate family, which also includes apes, humans, and lemurs. Monkeys have long tails that they use to hold on to things.

moss: tiny plants that grow in damp places, often on rocks or logs

mountains: large, rocky areas that are much higher than the land around them. The air on a mountain is often cool.

nutrients: the good things in food that animals' bodies need to survive

pouch: a pocket of skin on the front of a female marsupial animal where her baby feeds and grows

predator: an animal that lives by hunting and eating other animals

prey: an animal that is hunted by other animals

rain forest: a warm, wet forest with very tall trees

rodents: a group of small mammals that have sharp teeth and chew a lot. They include mice, beavers, and squirrels.

scales: tough, flat pieces of skin on the tails of beavers, and on the bodies of animals such as fish and snakes

shellfish: water animals with bodies covered in a shell. Shellfish include shrimp, lobsters, and clams.

termites: small insects that are related to ants

tusks: long, pointed teeth that grow out of an animal's face or mouth

waterproof: something that keeps water out. A raincoat is waterproof.

webbed: having a "web" of skin connecting the toes. A duck's feet are webbed.

wetlands: areas of land that are covered in water at least part of the time

Index

A

anteater, 8–9
antelope, 10–11, 24, 53, 84
apes, 26–27, 40–41, 50–51, 62–63
arctic hare, 12–13

B

baboon, 14–15, 53
bactrian camel, 22
bat, 34–35
bears, 42–43, 68–69
beaver, 16–17
black rhinoceros, 76
blue whale, 18–19
bottlenose dolphin, 29
buffalo, 20–21

C

camel, 22–23
caribou, 74–75
cats, 24–25, 52–55, 84–85
cheetah, 24–25
chimpanzee, 26–27

D

deer, 60–61, 74–75, 84
dolphin, 28–29, 64–65
dromedary camel, 22
duck-billed platypus, 30–31

E

elephant, 32–33

F

flying fox, 35
food, 4
fruit bat, 34–35

G

giant anteater, 8–9
giant panda, 36
giraffe, 38–39
golden lion tamarin, 83
gorilla, 40–41
gray seal, 79
grizzly bear, 42–43

H

habitats, 7
harp seal, 78
hippopotamus, 44–45

K

kangaroo, 46–47
koala, 48–49
kob antelope, 10

L

lemur, 50–51
leopard, 52–53
lion, 54–55, 93

M

mammal, definition of, 4
mandrill, 56–57
marsupials, 46–49
meerkat, 58–59
monkeys, 14–15, 50–51, 56–57, 80–83
moose, 60–61

O

orangutan, 62–63
orca, 28, 64–65
otter, 66–67

P

panda, 36–37
polar bear, 68–69
porcupine, 70–71

R

raccoon, 72–73
reindeer, 74–75, 91
rhinoceros, 76–77
ring-tailed lemur, 50–51
river otter, 66–67
rodents, 16–17, 70–71

S

sea otter, 66–67
seal, 65, 68, 78–79
snow monkey, 80–81
springbok, 11

T

tamarin, 82–83
tiger, 84–85

W

walrus, 86–87
warthog, 88–89
whale, 18–19
white rhinoceros, 76
wolf, 90–91

Z

zebra, 92–93